DATE DUE

The Library of SPIDERS™

The Orb Weaver

Alice B. McGinty

The Rosen Publishing Group's
PowerKids Press™
New York

For Zachary

Published in 2002 by the Rosen Publishing Group, Inc.
29 East 21st Street, New York, NY 10010

Copyright © 2002 by the Rosen Publishing Group, Inc.

First Edition

Book Design: Emily Muschinske
Project Editor: Emily Raabe
Project Consultant: Kathleen Reid Zeiders

Photo Credits: Title page, pp. 2, 3, 6, 21 (right and bottom) © David Liebman; p. 5 (top)
© Michael Fogden/Animals Animals; pp. 5 (bottom), 10, 11, 13, 14, 17, 18, 19, 21 (top)
© Robert Noonan; p. 9 (oval and bottom) © Bill Beatty/Animals Animals; p. 9 upper right
© Animals Animals.

McGinty, Alice B.
    The orb weaver / Alice B. McGinty.
        p. cm.— (The library of spiders)
    Includes index.
    Summary: This book introduces spiders known as "orb weavers," explaining their physical characteristics, their web making, and their reproduction.
        ISBN 0-8239-5569-9
        1. Araneidae—Juvenile literature. [1. Orb-weaving spiders. 2. Spiders.] I. Title. II. Series.
    QL458.42.A7 M44 2001
    595.4'4—dc21   00-011696

Manufactured in the United States of America.

Contents

4

The Orb Weaver

There are over 35,000 kinds of spiders in the world! Of all these spiders, orb weavers are probably the most well-known. Orb weavers live in every part of the world except Antarctica. They are known for their wheel-shaped webs, called orb webs.

Orb weavers come in many different sizes and shapes. Tiny orb weavers make orb webs small enough to fit between two blades of grass. Other orb weavers can be eight inches (20.3 cm) long with their legs stretched out. These big spiders can make orb webs that reach across wide streams.

(Top) This orb weaver has made a strong web out of zig zagging lines of silk.

(Bottom right) This is a wheel-shaped orb web.

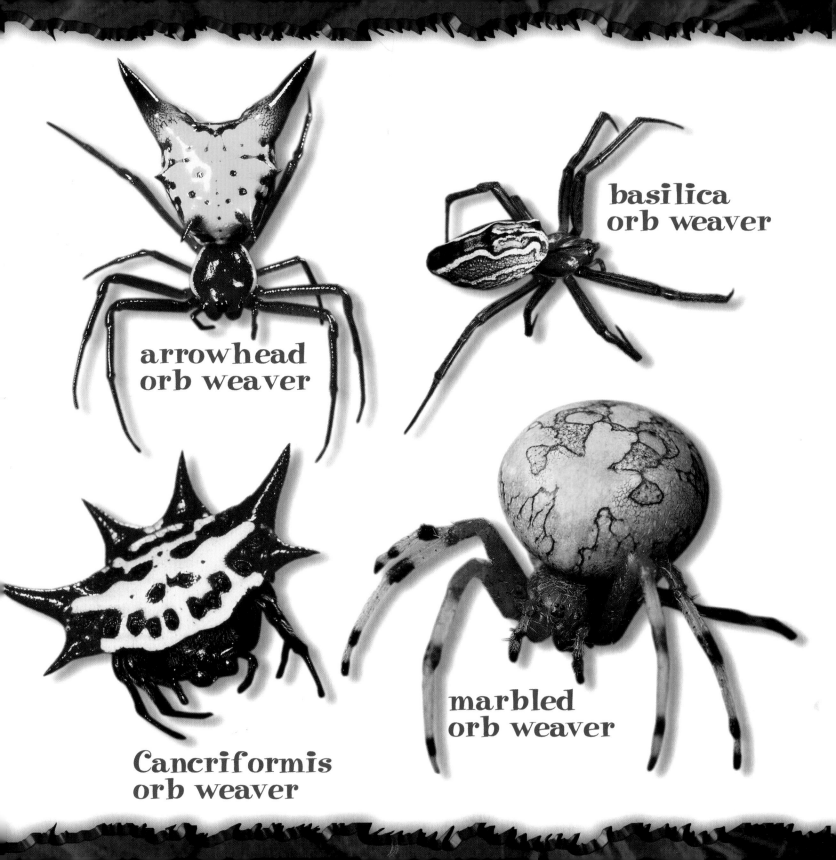

arrowhead
orb weaver

basilica
orb weaver

Cancriformis
orb weaver

marbled
orb weaver

Arachnids

Scientists place all plants and animals into groups so they can study them. All spiders are part of a group, or **class**, called **Arachnida**. Animals that are Arachnids have eight legs, two body parts, and no wings or **antennae**. Other arachnids include scorpions and mites.

The name Arachnida comes from a Greek **myth** about the creation of spiders. In the myth, a girl named Arachne beat the Greek goddess Athena in a weaving contest. The angry goddess tore up Arachne's weaving. Arachne was so upset that she killed herself. Athena felt sorry. She turned Arachne into a spider, so Arachne could keep weaving beautiful webs.

Most orb weavers belong to a smaller group, or **family**, of spiders called **Araneidae**. There are about 3,000 kinds, or **species**, of orb weavers in the family Araneidae.

(Left) Believe it or not, these spiders are all orb weavers!

The Orb Weaver's Body

Like all spiders, the orb weaver has two main body parts. The spider's front body part is called the **cephalothorax**. Inside the cephalothorax are the spider's brain and stomach. The spider's eight legs are attached to the cephalothorax.

The **abdomen** is the spider's rear body part. Inside it are the spider's heart, lungs, and silk **glands**. Orb weavers have large silk glands.

The orb weaver's body is covered with an **exoskeleton**. The exoskeleton is a hard shell that protects the spider's soft body.

(Bottom right) This shows a female (at left) and a male (at right) orb weaver.

(Below, left and right) Even though these two orb weavers look very different, you can see from the diagram that they have all the same body parts.

fangs

abdomen

silk glands

cephalothorax

(Above) This orb weaver is wrapping up its prey in strong silk.

(Left) This is a close-up photograph of the silk coming out of an orb weaver's spinnerettes.

Spinning Silk

The orb weaver's **spinnerettes** are on the back of its abdomen. Spinnerettes release silk. Silk comes out of the spinnerettes as a liquid. The spider tugs on the silk with its back legs. It blends the strands together into a solid thread.

Each spinnerette releases a different kind of silk. The orb weaver uses dry silk to make the strong edges of its web. It uses sticky silk around the middle of its web. Some orb weavers spin patterns of fuzzy silk on their webs too. Hairs and claws on the ends of their legs help orb weavers handle the silk. These hairs and claws keep orb weavers from getting stuck in their sticky webs.

(Right) This orb weaver used extra silk to build a thick cross into the web. The cross makes the web stronger.

The Orb Web

Orb webs can be found in gardens and grass, around trees, or in dark corners. When an orb weaver makes its web, it follows the same steps each time. The orb web takes about an hour to complete.

Many orb weavers build new webs each day. Orb weavers that catch **prey** at night build their webs as it gets dark. At dawn, the spider takes its old web down. It may eat its old web, so its body can use the **protein** from the old silk to make new silk. Bigger orb weavers do not replace their webs each day. They fix their webs if they are damaged.

(1) The orb weaver begins its web with a single drag line.
(2) The spider stretches threads from the center of the web towards the edges.
(3) The orb weaver strengthens its web by building a spiral out from the center of the web.
(4) The spider builds more and more spirals until its web is strong and complete.
(5) After catching a moth in its web, the spider quickly wraps it in silk. Then the orb weaver must repair the damage to its web.

Trapping Food

Orb weavers wait for insects to fly into their sticky webs. Some spiders hang upside down in the center of their webs. Others spin a special signal thread from the center of the web to a hideout where they wait nearby. When the signal thread vibrates, it tells the spider that an insect is caught in the web. The orb weaver runs onto its web. The orb weaver cannot see well. The tightness of the threads in its web tell the spider where the insect is.

The orb weaver wraps the insect in silk and bites it with its **fangs**. The spider's poison turns the insides of the insect to liquid. The spider sucks out the liquid until only the insect's shell is left.

(Left) These photographs show a moth getting stuck in an orb weaver's web. In the final picture (at right), the orb weaver sinks its fangs into the unlucky insect.

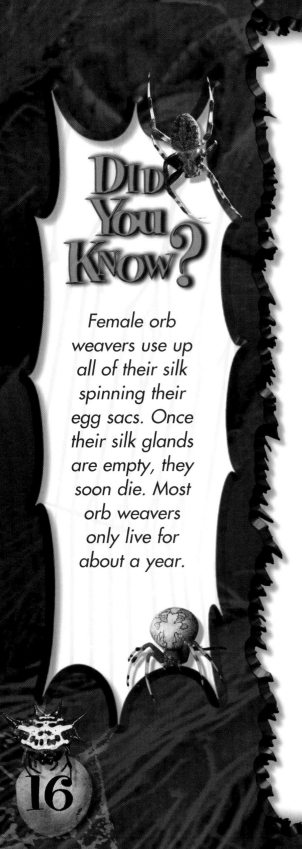

Laying Eggs

When a male orb weaver is full grown, he searches for a mate. He may spin a thread, called a mating thread, on the edge of a female's web. The male spider bounces and drums on the thread. The female spider feels the vibrations. If she is ready to mate, she joins the male spider on the mating thread.

Many female orb weavers lay their eggs in the fall. The female spider spins several silk bowls. She lays a few hundred eggs in each bowl. The spider rolls the bowls into silk egg sacs to keep them safe.

(Left) A male orb weaver approaches a female in order to mate with her.

(Below)
(1) The female, having mated with the male, builds a silk bowl in which to lay her eggs.

(2) The female lays her eggs into the silk bowl that she has built. The eggs are tiny dots in the yellow liquid.

(Top Left) This is a female orb weaver guarding her egg sac.

(Top Right) This is an older spiderling molting. It has wriggled out of its old skin and left the skin behind.

Baby Orb Weavers

An orb weaver's eggs usually hatch in the spring. Before the **spiderlings** come out of the egg sac, they shed their skin. This is called **molting**. After they molt, the spiderlings chew their way out of the egg sac. The growing spiderlings molt again when their hard exoskeletons become too small. They will molt many times before they are full grown.

Orb weaver spiderlings are born knowing how to make an orb web. The spiderlings might build a web and live together for a short time. Staying close together helps protect them from **predators**.

When they are ready to live on their own, the spiderlings climb up high. They spin strands of silk that catch the breeze and carry them away. This is called ballooning. The spiderlings will make their own webs wherever they land.

(Right) The tiny specks in this picture are spiderlings.

19

DID YOU KNOW?

Some unusual orb weavers, called social orb weavers, work together to stay safe. They build their webs close together, and they all stay together in a hideout nearby.

The Orb Weaver's Enemies

Wasps, frogs, lizards, birds, and other spiders all eat orb weavers. Orb weavers protect themselves from predators in many ways.

The spider's first response to a predator is to hide. It may attach a safety line called a dragline to its web and lower itself to the ground. When it is on the ground, the spider pulls its legs in and lies still.

Some orb weavers shake their webs violently when predators come near. This makes it hard for the predator to see the spider. If the predator can not see the spider clearly, it can not attack.

(Left) This orb weaver is swinging from its dragline.

(Below) This shows an orb weaver shaking its web to confuse predators.

(Below) This wasp is trying to lay its egg on a spider's egg sac. If the wasp succeeds, the young wasp will hatch and eat the spider's eggs.

Orb Weavers and People

Orb webs are not only beautiful, but are also helpful to people. Some orb webs trap more than 100 insects each day. It has been said that without the help of spiders, insects would take over the world!

The silk of the golden orb weaver has been used by people in many ways. The U.S. government has even thought about using it to make bulletproof vests. Golden orb silk is strong and hard to break. It can stretch to absorb the force of a bullet. Golden orb webs have also been collected and used as fishing nets by people who fish on tropical islands.

If you find an orb web, look at it carefully. You might be lucky enough to see the amazing spider that built it!

Glossary

abdomen (AB-duh-min) A spider's rear body part.

antennae (ann-TEN-YE) Two feelers that are part of an insect's body.

Arachnida (eh-RACK-nid-da) The class of arthropods that are arachnids, or animals with four pairs of legs and two body segments. Spiders and scorpions are in the class Arachnida.

Araneidae (ayr-uh-NAY-ih-dee) The family of spiders that includes most orb weavers.

cephalothorax (sef-uh-low-THOR-ax) A spider's front body part made up of its head and chest.

class (KLASS) A group, larger than a family, in which scientists place plants or animals that are similar in some ways.

exoskeleton (ek-oh-SKEH-lah-ton) The hard outer shell of a spider's body.

family (FAM-ih-lee) A group in which scientists place animals or plants that are similar in some ways.

fangs (FANGZ) Hollow teeth that inject venom.

glands (GLANDZ) A part inside the body that takes a substance from the blood and changes it into a chemical that the body gives off.

molting (MOHLT-ing) Shedding the outer layer of skin or hair.

myth (MITH) A traditional story, usually about gods, goddesses, or heroes, that often explains something about the world.

predators (PREH-duh-terz) Animals that kill other animals for food.

prey (PRAY) An animal that is hunted by another animal for food.

protein (PROH-teen) A substance inside the cells of people, plants, and animals.

species (SPEE-sheez) A single kind of plant or animal. All people are one species.

spinnerettes (spin-uhr-ETZ) Organs that are located on the rear of the spider's abdomen and that release silk.

Index

Web Sites

For more information about orb weavers and other spiders check out these Web sites:

http://entowww.tamu.edu/extension/youth/bug/bug163.html
http://naturalpartners.org/InsectZoo/Students/araneae.html
www.ufsia.ac.be/Arachnology/Pages/Kids.html